The
NYSTROM
Nystronaut ATLAS

Hello, Earthling! We're the Nystronauts.

Help us learn about your world's communities.

And we will help you learn about maps.

NYSTROM
HERFF JONES EDUCATION DIVISION

This list is called the table of contents.

Contents

A Picture Atlas of Communities · 4–17

Learning About Globes and Maps · 18–23

Educational Consultant: Dr. JoAnne Buggey

2006 Update of Names and Boundaries
Copyright © 2005, 1998 NYSTROM Herff Jones Education Division
3333 Elston Avenue, Chicago, Illinois 60618

10 9 8 7 6 5 4 3 2   12 11 10 09 08 07 06

ISBN: 0-7825-1051-5   Product Code Number: 9A97B

For information about ordering this atlas, call toll-free 800-621-8086.

Printed in U.S.A.

You can get lots of help on the final pages.

Where do you live?

Wow! There's your world in the distance.

A This is how the earth looks from above the moon.

Closer in, we can pick out your country.

B The yellow outline shows the United States. It was added to the photo.

Closer yet! Now we can pick out states.

C Here the yellow outline shows state boundary lines.

If we zoom in, we can see how Earthlings live.

D This community and yours are not exactly the same. But they are alike in many ways.

Which community is like

Communities come in many sizes. Some are big cities. Others are very small.

A Big cities have many people and workplaces.

How tall are the buildings in YOUR community?

B Suburbs are located near big cities.

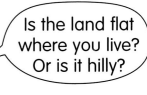

Is the land flat where you live? Or is it hilly?

C Towns are smaller than cities and have fewer people.

Which of these communities looks most like yours?

How are they alike?

D Farms and their neighbors are communities too.

What kinds of places can

This community has places to live, work, learn, and shop. So do most other communities.

A Office buildings are where many people provide services.

Find the places in the photos on the map.

B Flower stores are where florists sell flowers.

C Schools are where students learn.

D Houses are where people live.

E Grocery stores are where people buy food.

Do you live near places like these? Which ones?

F Factories are where many people make goods.

How do people help

People help others in their community. Working together makes a community better.

We learn to help at home.

A Brothers and their mother make dinner together.

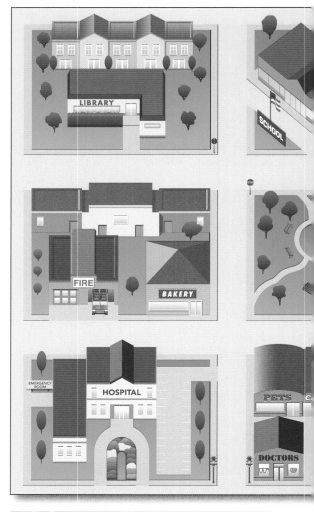

B Children line up to let everyone have a turn.

C Team members help each other win the game.

Where do people help each other?

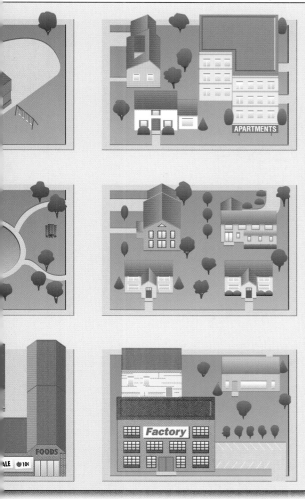

D Hospital workers help people who are hurt.

F Children clean the beach.

E Young adults feed people who are hungry.

What services do

Many people provide services for the whole community. Some of them work in the town hall.

A Firefighters put out fires and save lives.

B Garbage collectors keep the community clean.

Who else helps the community?

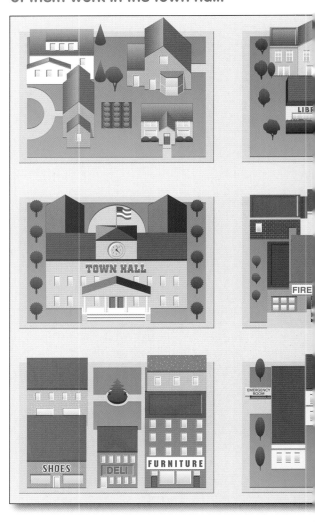

C Librarians help people find books for learning and fun.

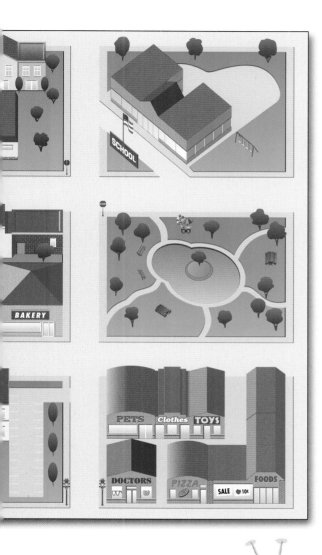

D Police officers keep everyone safe.

E Judges settle serious disagreements.

Find a place on the map where a crossing guard works.

F Crossing guards help children cross the street.

What do people make

Many communities have factories. But factories are not the only places where goods are made.

A Baby food is made in a factory.

What does that stuff taste like?

B Sometimes furniture is made in a workshop.

C Televisions are made in a factory.

D Medicines are made in a laboratory.

E These baskets are made in this woman's home.

Which people are working in factories?

What do you mean by "factory"?

F Sometimes dresses are made in a workshop.

What do people buy here?

Green food looks fun to eat! Is it good for you?

People satisfy some of their needs and wants by buying goods and services in stores and offices.

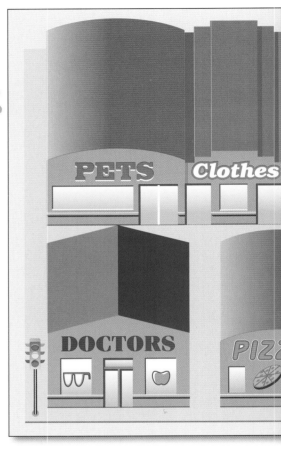

A People go to grocery stores to buy food.

B Adults visit the pharmacy to buy medicine.

C Teenagers go to the box office to buy movie tickets.

Do Earthlings pay for dental care and other services?

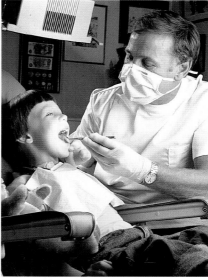

D Children see the dentist to get their teeth checked.

E Families shop at clothing stores for things to wear.

Can you find places like these on the map?

F This girl and her father visit a toy store to buy a doll.

What view does

Find this library in views B, C, and D.

A Most of the time you see buildings in a **view from the ground.**

B At an angle in flight, you get a **bird's-eye view.**

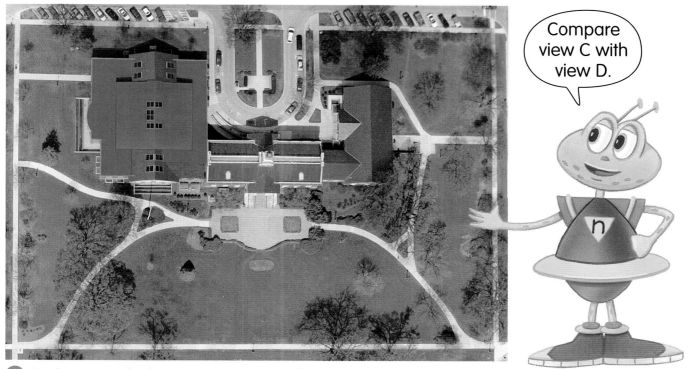

Compare view C with view D.

C Looking straight down, you get a **view from directly above.**

How is the map like the photo?

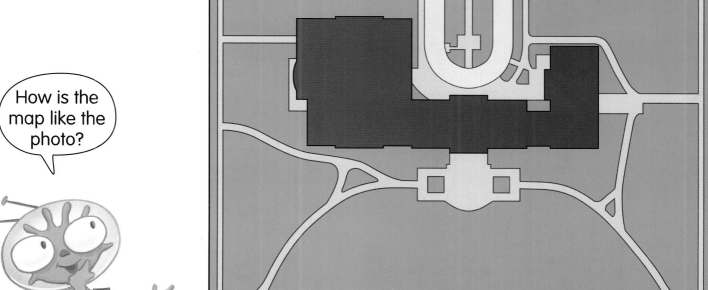

D A **map view** is a special drawing of a place seen from directly above.

How do maps show real

A **Coastlines** are shown as black lines between land and ocean features.

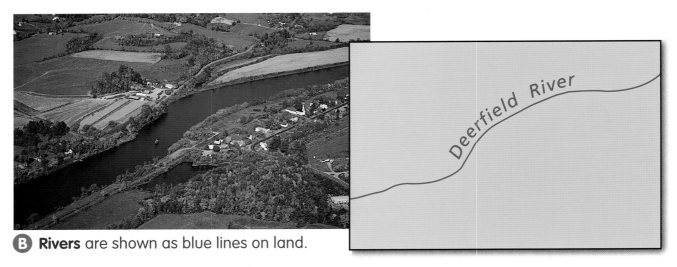

B **Rivers** are shown as blue lines on land.

C **Lakes** are shown as blue areas surrounded by land.

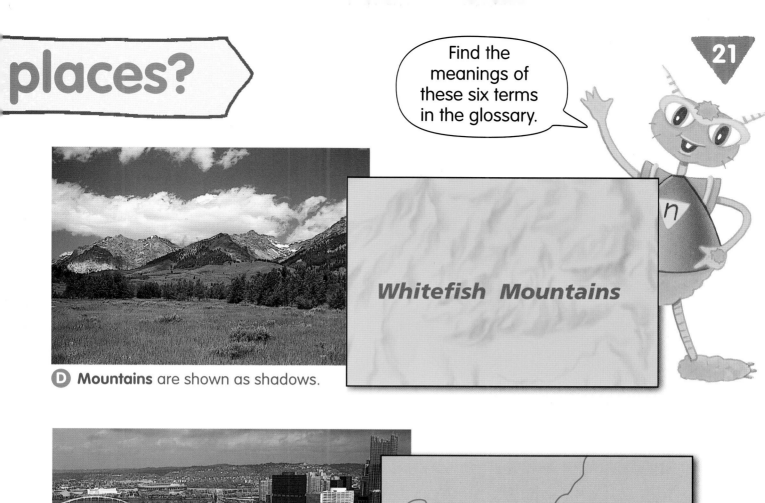

places?

Find the meanings of these six terms in the glossary.

Whitefish Mountains

D **Mountains** are shown as shadows.

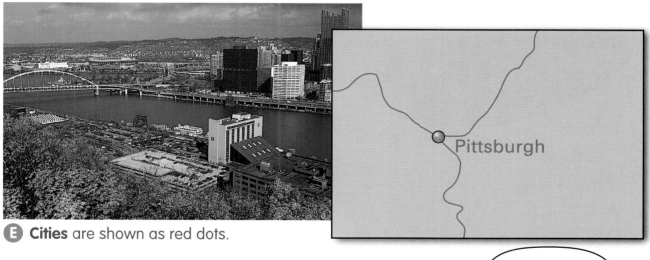

E **Cities** are shown as red dots.

Pittsburgh

On the ground, you see a sign, not a line!

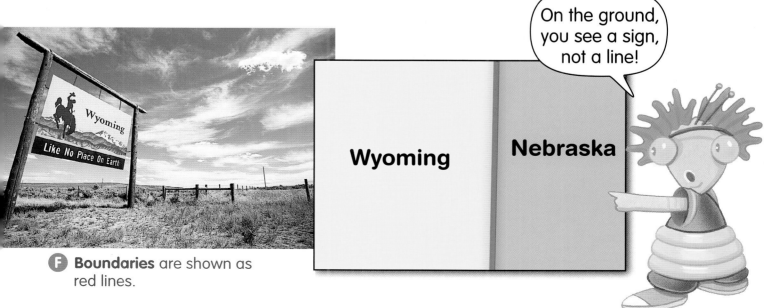

Wyoming

Wyoming

Nebraska

F **Boundaries** are shown as red lines.

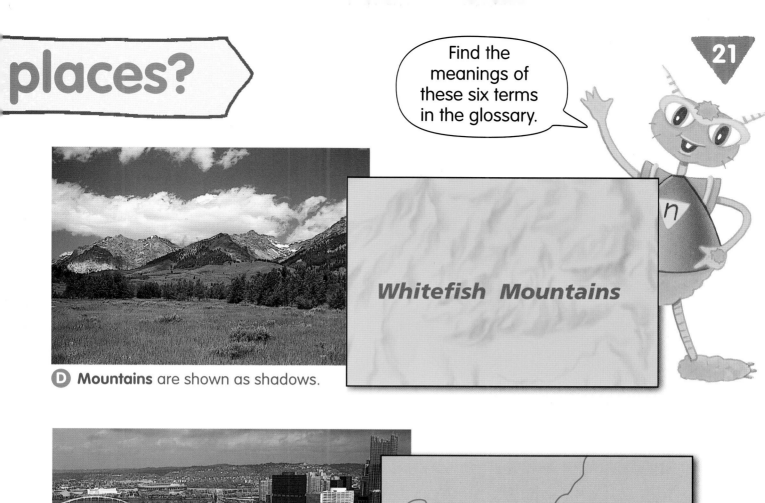

places?

Find the meanings of these six terms in the glossary.

Whitefish Mountains

D **Mountains** are shown as shadows.

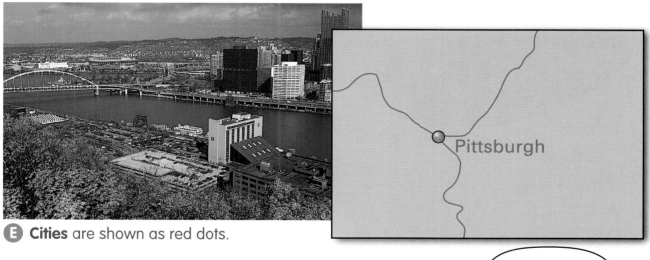

E **Cities** are shown as red dots.

Pittsburgh

On the ground, you see a sign, not a line!

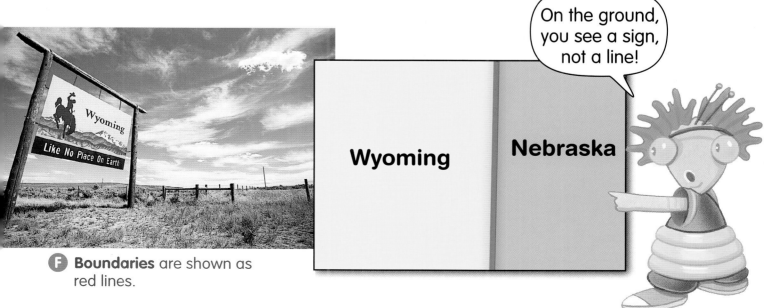

Wyoming | **Nebraska**

F **Boundaries** are shown as red lines.

How do globes and

Now it's our turn to help you read maps and globes.

A The earth looks like this from space.

Is the earth round like a penny or round like a ball?

B A globe is a model of the earth.

Which is easier to read: a map or a peeled globe?

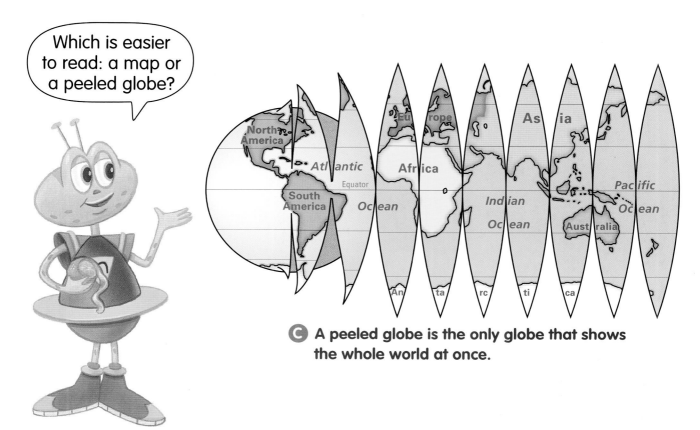

C A peeled globe is the only globe that shows the whole world at once.

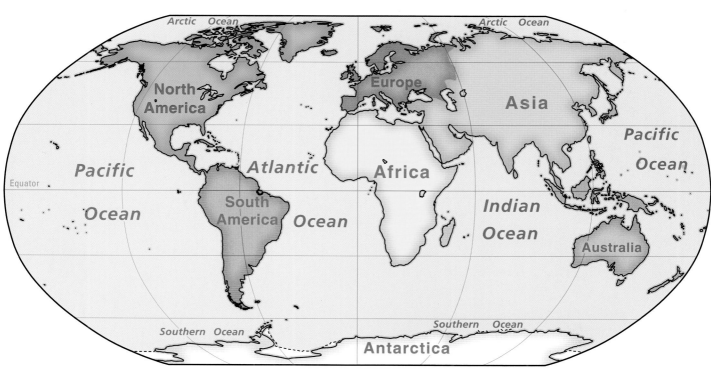

D Any world map can show the whole world at once.

What do the different colors show?

Arctic Ocean

Greenland (Denmark)

Russia

Alaska (United States)

Canada
North America

United States

Mexico

Cuba

Puerto Rico (United States)

Atlantic

Guatemala

Nicaragua

Panama

Venezuela

Colombia

Hawaii (United States)

Pacific

Ocean

Equator

South America

Peru

Brazil

Bolivia

Argentina

Chile

Ocean

Southern Ocean

Uni King

Ireland

Morocc

Mauritania

Senegal

Guinea

N
W E
S

World

North America	Continent
United States	Country
Alaska	State, territory
Indian Ocean	Ocean feature
○○○○○○○○○○○○	Continental boundary
——————	Country boundary
	Mountains

Scale in miles at the Equator

0   1000   2000

1 inch stands for 1580 miles

Where is your state?

Name the places near your state.

United States

Canada	Country
Arizona	State
● New York City	City
⊛ Washington, D.C.	Country capital
★ Denver	State capital
Rocky Mountains	Land feature
Atlantic Ocean	Ocean feature
Mississippi River	River, lake
▬▬▬▬▬	Country boundary
▬▬▬▬▬	State boundary
	Mountains

Scale in miles

0   100   200   300   400

1 inch stands for 225 miles

How do citizens help

A Citizens vote to pick their leaders.

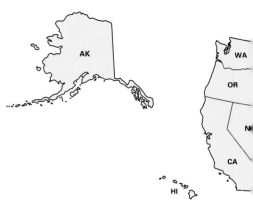

Citizens in every state use their rights and perform their responsibilities. In both ways they help run our country and keep it safe.

B Citizens on a jury make the final decision in a trial.

How does someone become a citizen?

C Citizens pay taxes that provide roads and other government services.

Washington, D.C.

D Citizens in the military protect our country.

Mayor and president are public offices.

E Citizens can try to win election to public office.

F Almost any citizen can become president.

People in the photos show how people lived long ago. Match letters to find each photo's place on the map.

A 1500 and earlier Navajos and other Native Americans were the only people in the Americas.

Did they make everything themselves?

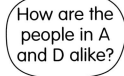

How are the people in A and D alike?

B 1600s British settlers started colonies at Jamestown and other places in the East.

C 1700s Spanish priests built missions in California that served as churches, schools, and towns.

D 1800s Many pioneer families moved west, built their own houses, and made their own goods.

What was YOUR community like long ago?

1490	1769–1823	1959
Only Native Americans live in the Americas.	Spain builds missions in California.	The United States adds its 50th state.

1500	1600	1700	1800	1900	2000

	1607		1776		Today
	Britain starts a colony in Virginia.		The United States declares independence on July 4.		What is our country like now?

F People from many places settled in the United States.

How do we use natural

See how wood comes from forests.

Natural resources are materials from nature that people use. Wood is one example.

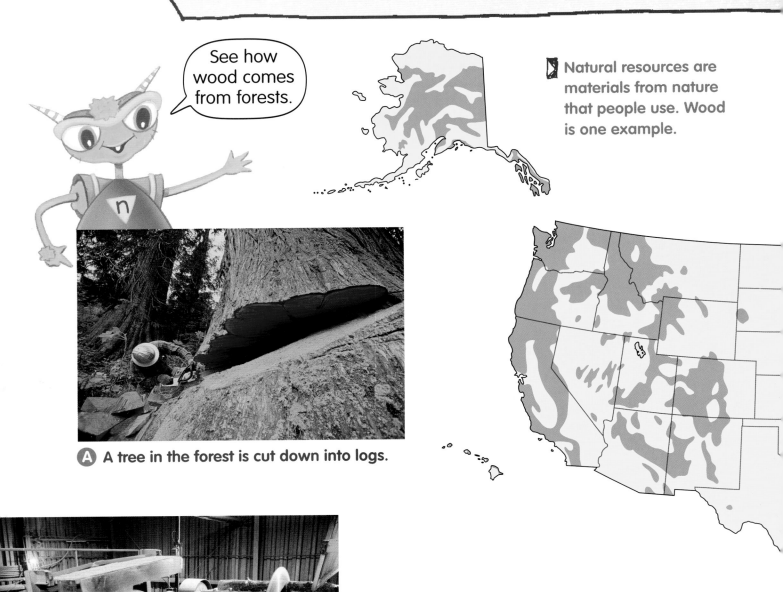

A A tree in the forest is cut down into logs.

B Logs in a sawmill are cut into boards.

C Boards are used to build a house.

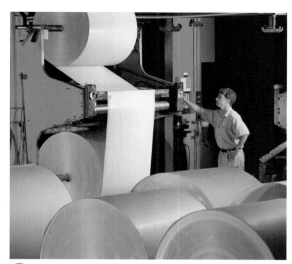

D Wood is used for making paper.

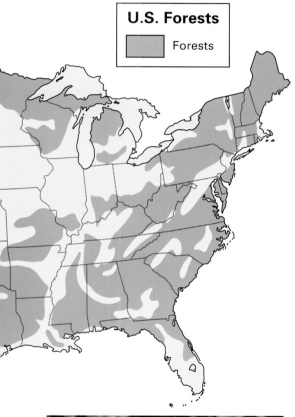

U.S. Forests

Forests

E Wood is used for certain musical instruments.

F Wood is used for furniture too.

What other goods are made of wood?

What do people do in

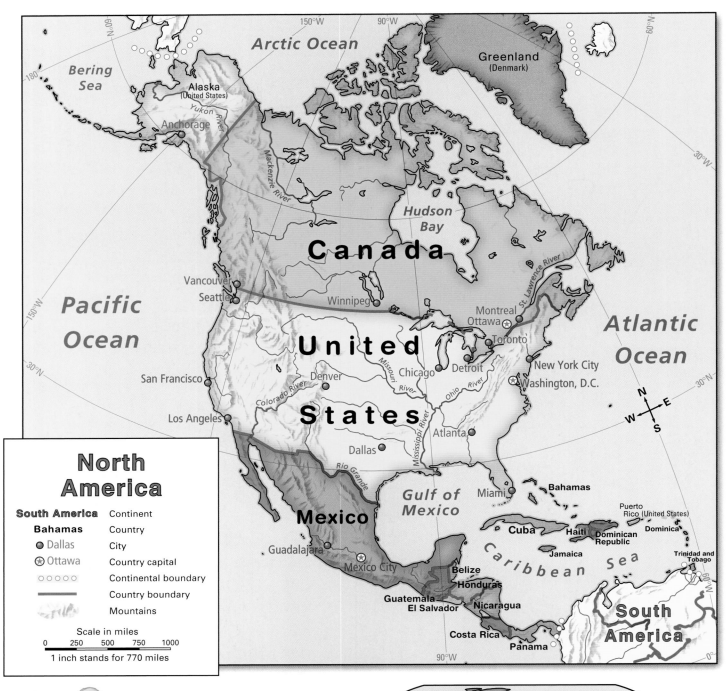

Arctic Ocean

Bering Sea

Greenland (Denmark)

Alaska (United States)

Yukon River

Anchorage

Mackenzie River

Hudson Bay

C a n a d a

St. Lawrence River

Pacific Ocean

Vancouver
Seattle

Winnipeg

Montreal
Ottawa

Atlantic Ocean

Toronto

U n i t e d

Chicago
Detroit

New York City
Washington, D.C.

San Francisco

Denver

Missouri River

Ohio River

N
W — E
S

S t a t e s

Colorado River

Atlanta

Los Angeles

Dallas

Mississippi River

Rio Grande

Gulf of Mexico

Miami

Bahamas

Puerto Rico (United States)

Mexico

Cuba
Haiti
Dominican Republic
Dominica

Guadalajara

Jamaica

Trinidad and Tobago

Mexico City

Belize

C a r i b b e a n   S e a

Honduras

Guatemala
El Salvador
Nicaragua

South America

Costa Rica
Panama

North America

South America	Continent
Bahamas	Country
● Dallas	City
✪ Ottawa	Country capital
○○○○○	Continental boundary
——	Country boundary
	Mountains

Scale in miles
0   250   500   750   1000
1 inch stands for 770 miles

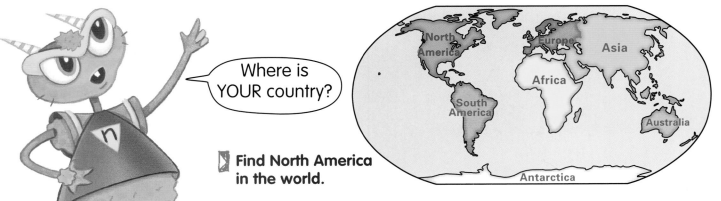

Where is YOUR country?

North America
Europe
Asia
Africa
South America
Australia
Antarctica

▷ **Find North America in the world.**

A A woman in Guatemala buys fresh bananas.

B A girl in Alaska bounces with help from her friends.

C A family in Mexico makes masks for the Day of the Dead holiday.

> Use the map to find the places in the photos.

D Cowboys in Cuba herd their cattle.

E Bike riders in Canada rest after a long ride.

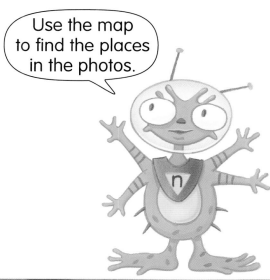

What do people do in

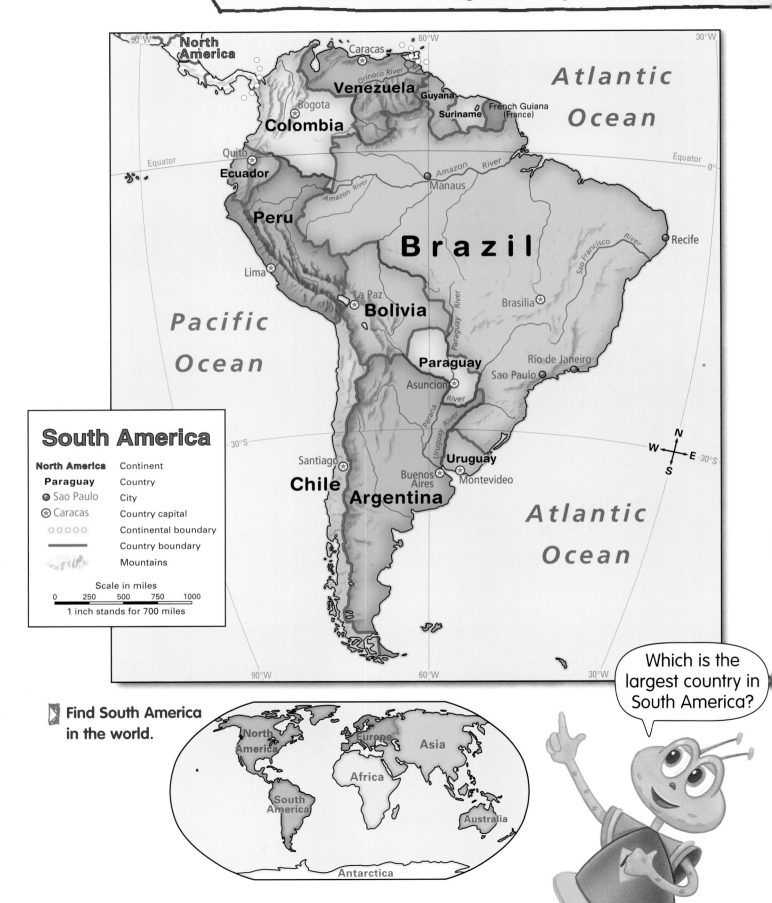

South America

North America	Continent
Paraguay	Country
● Sao Paulo	City
✹ Caracas	Country capital
○○○○○	Continental boundary
——	Country boundary
	Mountains

Scale in miles

0   250   500   750   1000

1 inch stands for 700 miles

Find South America
in the world.

Which is the
largest country in
South America?

A These men in Bolivia play wooden flutes.

B A woman in Colombia picks coffee beans.

C A boy in Peru takes care of his family's alpaca.

Does your family have any animals?

D These men in Brazil sell bananas for shipment around the world.

E Sisters and their mother take a walk in a park in Argentina.

What do people do in

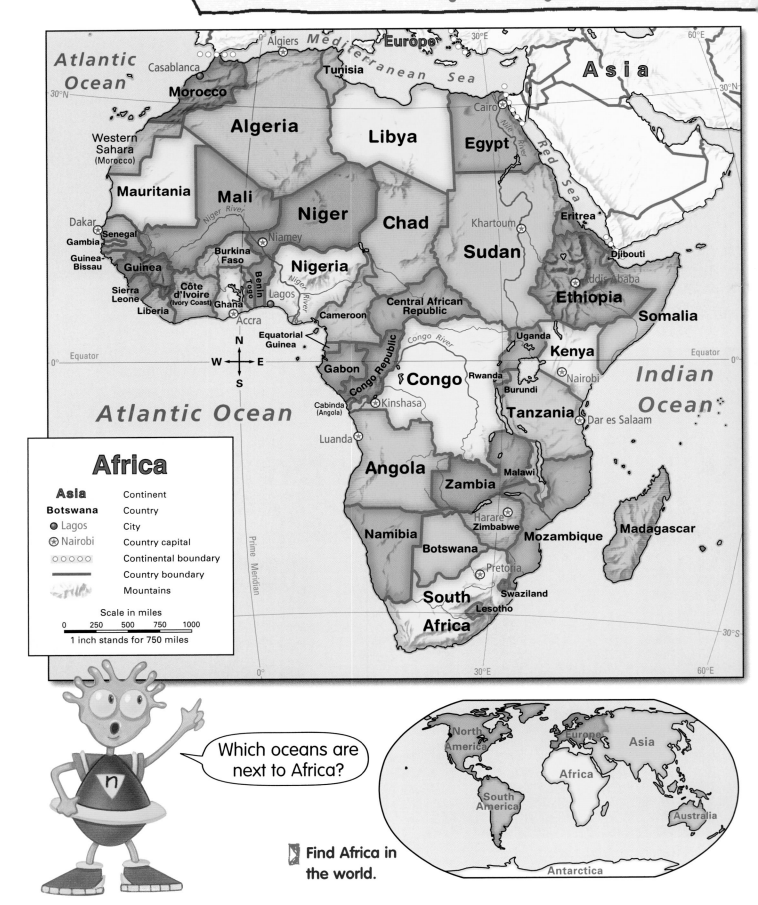

Atlantic Ocean

Mediterranean Sea

Europe

Asia

Algiers · Tunisia

Casablanca

Morocco

Algeria

Libya

Cairo

Egypt

Nile River

Red Sea

Western Sahara (Morocco)

Mauritania

Mali

Niger

Chad

Khartoum

Eritrea

Dakar · Senegal

Niger River

Niamey

Sudan

Djibouti

Gambia

Burkina Faso

Addis Ababa

Guinea-Bissau

Guinea

Nigeria

Niger River

Ethiopia

Sierra Leone

Côte d'Ivoire (Ivory Coast)

Benin Togo

Lagos

Central African Republic

Somalia

Liberia

Ghana

Accra

Cameroon

Uganda

Kenya

Equator

Equatorial Guinea

Congo River

Nairobi

Indian Ocean

N
W E
S

Gabon

Congo Republic

Congo

Rwanda
Burundi

Atlantic Ocean

Cabinda (Angola)

Kinshasa

Dar es Salaam

Tanzania

Luanda

Angola

Zambia

Malawi

Prime Meridian

Namibia

Harare
Zimbabwe

Mozambique

Madagascar

Botswana

Pretoria

South Africa

Swaziland

Lesotho

Africa

Asia	Continent
Botswana	Country
● Lagos	City
⊛ Nairobi	Country capital
○○○○○	Continental boundary
——	Country boundary
〰〰〰	Mountains

Scale in miles

0   250   500   750   1000

1 inch stands for 750 miles

Which oceans are next to Africa?

North America

Europe

Asia

Africa

South America

Australia

Antarctica

▶ Find Africa in the world.

A Men in Egypt enjoy a game of dominoes.

How does YOUR family get to the store?

D A family in Mali goes to the local market.

B This woman in South Africa shops in a supermarket.

C Children in Sudan come home from school.

E A woman in Botswana polishes diamonds.

A A woman in Russia sells fresh vegetables.

B A family in the United Kingdom enjoys the beach.

Can a country be in two continents?

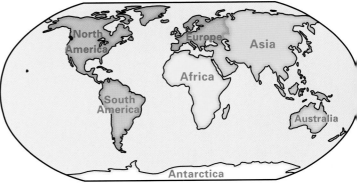

Find Europe in the world.

Europe

Asia	Continent
Ukraine	Country
◉ Istanbul	City
✪ Berlin	Country capital
○○○○○	Continental boundary
――――	Country boundary
	Mountains

Scale in miles

0   250   500   750

1 inch stands for 425 miles

What ocean did these fish come from?

C Fishermen in Portugal net a big catch.

D A hiker in Switzerland examines flowers.

E Sisters in France take bread home.

A Farmers in India sell their vegetables.

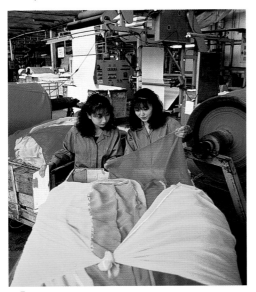

B Workers in Japan check cloth from their factory.

Are any continents larger than Asia?

Find Asia in the world.

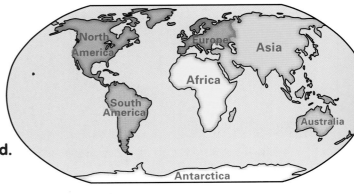

Asia

Africa	Continent
Thailand	Country
⬤ Karachi	City
✪ Baghdad	Country capital
○○○○○○	Continental boundary
———	Country boundary
〰️	Mountains

Scale in miles

0   250   500   750   1000

1 inch stands for 950 miles

C A girl in Mongolia plays while her family makes rope.

D A father in Saudi Arabia helps his son with homework.

Where do you do YOUR homework?

E Young women in Thailand perform a traditional dance.

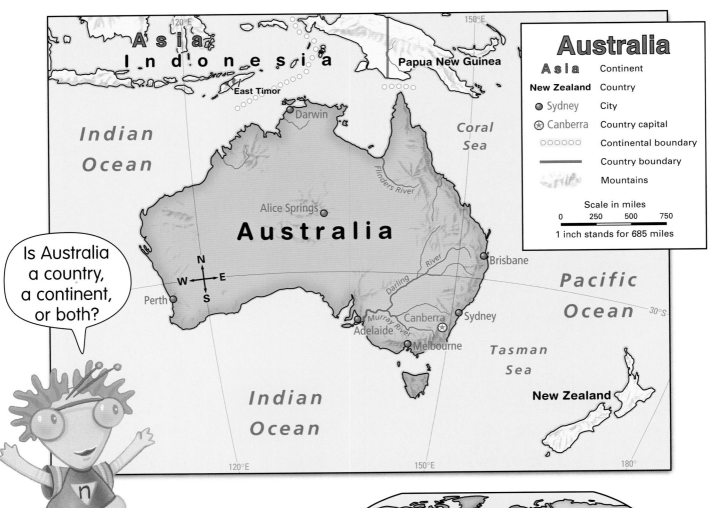

Asia
Indonesia
East Timor
Papua New Guinea
Darwin
Indian
Ocean
Coral
Sea
Flinders River
Alice Springs
Australia
N
W E
S
Perth
Darling River
Murray River
Adelaide
Canberra
Melbourne
Brisbane
Sydney
Pacific
Ocean
30°S
Tasman
Sea
Indian
Ocean
New Zealand
120°E
150°E
180°

Australia

Asia	Continent
New Zealand	Country
● Sydney	City
⊛ Canberra	Country capital
○○○○○○	Continental boundary
———	Country boundary
	Mountains

Scale in miles
0   250   500   750
1 inch stands for 685 miles

Is Australia a country, a continent, or both?

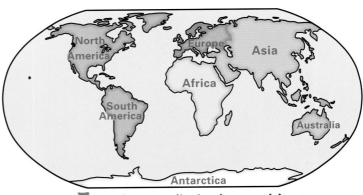

North America
Europe
Asia
Africa
South America
Australia
Antarctica

📎 **Find Australia in the world.**

Ⓐ **A family flies kites near Melbourne.**

Ⓑ **An artist in Alice Springs paints cloth.**

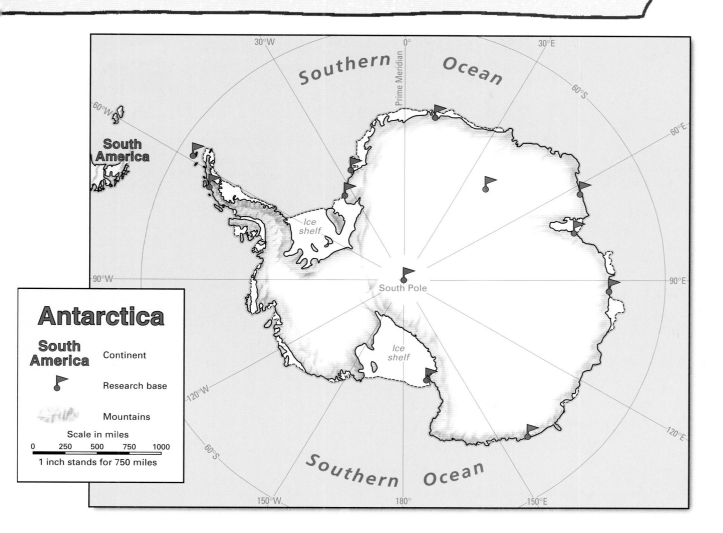

Antarctica

South America	Continent
▶ (flag)	Research base
(shaded)	Mountains

Scale in miles

0   250   500   750   1000

1 inch stands for 750 miles

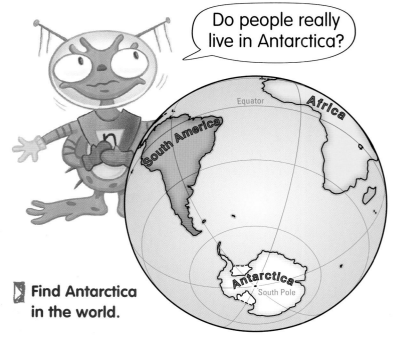

Do people really live in Antarctica?

Find Antarctica in the world.

C A tourist in Antarctica watches a penguin.

Glossary

A glossary tells what words mean.

atlas A book of maps.

boundary Where two states, countries, or continents meet. It is shown on a map as a line or a row of dots.

capital City where the government of a country or state is located.

citizen Person who is a member of his or her country.

city Place where many people live and work. A city is bigger than a town.

coastline The edge of a continent or island along a sea or an ocean.

community An area where people live. Places in a neighborhood are within walking distance of each other.

compass rose A set of arrows on a map that point north, south, east, and west.

compass rose

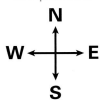

continent One of the seven largest land areas.

continents

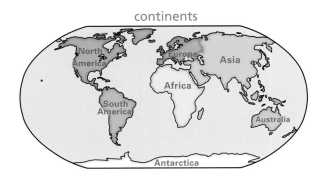

country A land with one government. Some countries have many states.

Equator Imaginary line around the middle of the earth. The Equator is the same distance from the North Pole and the South Pole.

Equator

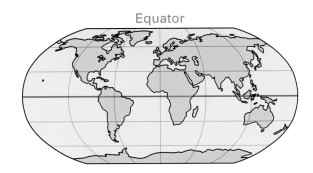

factory Building where a company makes goods.

farm Place where crops are grown, animals are raised for food, or both.

forest Area covered by trees.

globe A model of the earth that is round like a ball.

goods Products that can be bought and sold.

lake A body of water, usually fresh. The water in a lake stays in one place.

map A special drawing of all or part of the earth as seen from above. A map uses symbols and colors to show where places are located.

model Three-dimensional copy of an object or a place. A model is made at a size that is easy to study or play with.

mountain Part of the earth that is much taller than the land around it. A mountain is like a hill, but much larger and higher.

natural resource Something found in nature that is used by people.

needs Things that make it possible to live.

North Pole Imaginary point that is farther north than any other place on earth.

ocean One of the five large, salty bodies of water that cover most of the earth.

oceans

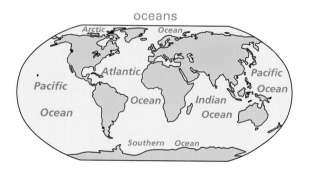

Prime Meridian Imaginary line from the North Pole to the South Pole. The Prime Meridian passes through London in the United Kingdom.

Prime Meridian

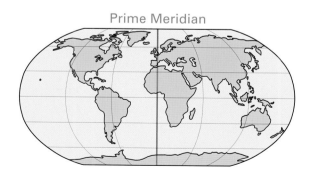

river A long, narrow body of water. The water in a river flows downhill.

sea Part of the ocean that has its own name. A sea is usually located near land.

services Jobs that help people.

settler Person who moves into an area to live.

South Pole Imaginary point that is farther south than any other place on earth.

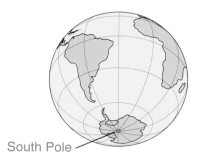

state Part of a country. A state has a governor and laws of its own. There are 50 states in the United States of America.

All these words are used in the atlas.

suburb Town or small city located near a big city. Most big cities have many suburbs.

town Place where people live and work. A town is smaller than a city.

wants Things that make life more fun.

Does this index list YOUR country?

Index